Chers Amis

Chers

Amis

photographs and text

by **Janet Belden Beyda**

with the collaboration of Frank Beyda

with an Introduction by Nicholas Meyer

Pomerica Press Limited
New York

Pomerica Press titles are distributed in the United States
by E. P. Dutton & Co., Inc.
201 Park Avenue South, New York, N.Y. 10003
and in Canada by Clarke, Irwin & Co., Ltd.,
791 St. Clair Ave. W., Toronto, Ont. M6C 1B8

Original French edition © 1976 Hier et Demain, Paris
Photographs © Frank Beyda
English-language edition © 1977 by Pomerica Press Limited
Library of Congress Catalog Card No. 77-848-75
ISBN 0-918732-01-8

Printed in the United States of America
10 9 8 7 6 5 4 3 2 1

to Topolino and Dizzy

Introduction

My dictionary defines anthropomorphism as the attribution of human temperamental characteristics to inanimate objects or to animals. At least, I assume it does; at any rate, that's what anthropomorphism means to me, and when I use a word, said the caterpillar to Alice. . . . There is no point in going to my dictionary to find the word that means attribution of animal characteristics to human beings, because my dictionary does not believe in antonyms.

It does not make a great deal of difference. Since the dawn of time, men have noticed their own characteristics in animals (we presumptuously take them to be *our* characteristics, not theirs) and vice versa. The latter comparison is scarcely deemed a flattering one (e.g. "You beast!") is obviously intended as some sort of compliment. (There is an old maxim," wrote Mark Twain, "that Man is the noblest work of God. Now who found that out?")

Ancient Egyptians stuck bird heads on the human bodies of their gods, and, even-handed, gave to the Sphinx's lion body a woman's head. For all I know, or suspect, the Egyptians were not even first to practice this artistically suggestive mismatching. As evidenced by this book of photographs, they were certainly not the last.

The theater and the movies have played around a good deal with the idea of anthropomorphism. No doubt, Shakespeare in *A Midsummer Night's Dream,* intended Bottom, wooed in his ass's head by the fair Titania, as high comedy. The fact remains that most of us find their scenes together, and the many artistic representations of them, oddly touching as well as amusing. Similarly, the French fairy tale, *La Belle et la Bête,* tells of another quaintly romantic couple. (It is interesting to note that when Greta Garbo saw Jean Cocteau's film adaptation of the story, she sighed with disappointment when the beast was transformed into the handsome prince and murmured plaintively, "Give me back my beast." A lot of us, for reasons we probably could not explain, have felt the same way.)

The Wizard of Oz gave Americans a Cowardly Lion to think about and most of the film version's enthusiastic following might claim that Bert Lahr's Cowardly Lion steals the picture from the incredible Judy Garland. But then, how often have we heard actors bemoan the fact that it is impossible to steal any scene from an animal?

In addition to the benign aspects of anthropo-morphism, there are also the terrible. And here,

Hollywood has had a fine old time. Where else, but through the magic of make-up and special effects, would it be possible to watch with mounting horror the actual transformation from man to beast? Henry Hull and Lon Chaney are forever printed on the minds of those who witnessed their shocking degeneration.

Perhaps the most terrifying and dramatic example of species interchange occurs in Homer, where the crew of Odysseus is betwitched in the palace of the enchantress, Circe, and are metamorphosed into swine.

Children's literature abounds with anthropomorphic heroes and heroines. What does this fascination with anthropomorphic heroes and heroines, and the other way around, mean? Since the beginning of human time, mankind has shared the planet with animals.

We have hunted them and befriended them, tamed them and abused them, taught them and fought them, exploited them, raised them, and even eaten them. They have provided us with shelter, nutrition, clothing, companionship, and transportation. Yet until recently, we have known very little about our partners in history. Specifically, we do not know about their thoughts, but we do know they have souls: we have seen animals grieve, rejoice, rage, and respond to affection.

But what do they think? And perhaps more specifically, what do they think of us? Our various projections veer back and forth, between the benign and the satanic. If we could settle the issue once and for all, perhaps the topic would bore us.

But we cannot. Or have not yet. Hence, the perennial fascination as evidenced, most recently, by this collection of ingenious, provocative, and sometimes disturbing photographs.

What do these pictures make you think of?

Nicholas Meyer

We of the animal world are happy to be released from the abstractions you have imposed on us for so long. The lion has had enough of being a symbol of strength, the fox of cunning, the goose of stupidity, the pig of slovenliness, the snake of perfidy. Thanks to the more perceptive eye of the camera, you can now understand us as individuals and accept us as friends.

As you see, we are having certain difficulties in adjusting our Egos to our Ids, and both of them to the situations we encounter in our daily life. We are looking to you, with your superior knowledge of psychiatry, to come to our assistance.

PORTRAIT OF FRANK BEYDA & JANET BELDEN

Lola Lananni is one of the most recent film finds. Her first vehicle, "The Cart", has attracted the attention of all the leading critics, who predict a career comparable to that of Greta Garbo or Marilyn Monroe.

Her unusual type brings a fresh personality to the screen ; and her name an assonance that has not been heard since the days of Lillie Langtry.

When Judge Simeon Socrates was admitted to the bar in 1921 he was outstanding as having the highest ambitions and the lowest grades on record.

His untiring efforts to raise the latter to the level of the former have so stimulated his gray matter that his wig has been growing longer and longer, to the point where it alone constitutes an impressive costume. He is now known in legal circles as His Honor Sans-Culotte.

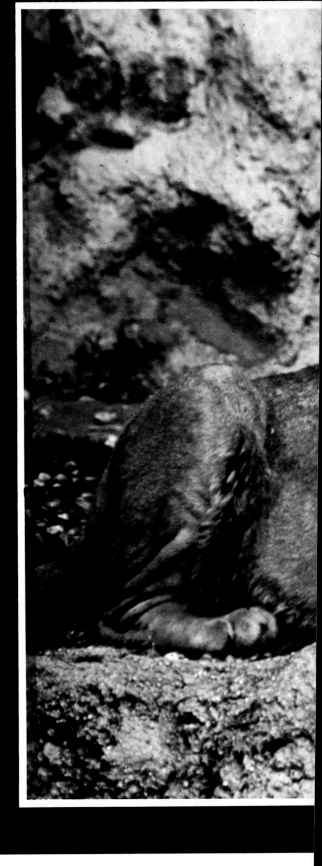

Uncle Leo believed that what he lacked was not perspicacity but 20/20 vision and he is very pleased to discover that his surmise was correct. With his new glasses he can see right through everyone in the family...

...he can even see the point of a joke before you get to it.

He has few friends.

When Jean-Pierre grew to doghood, he had so much difficulty in
keeping a job that he was finally sent to an analyst, who
quickly discovered his problem: he had been brought up in a home
where he was told so often to "Stay put!" that staying put
became an ingrained habit—one little adapted to almost any kind
of work.

However the story has a happy ending because he joined the
National Guard and can now be seen any day proudly
staying put in front of the President's palace:

Our roving reporter recently interviewed Monsieur R. Solomon, one of the biggest egg merchants in France, on the subject of the new bill proposed by the leaders of the HLM (Hen-Lib Movement).

Reporter : *"What do you think of obligatory monogamy ?"*
M. Solomon : *"Unthinkable ! It would play havoc with our present economy."*

"I'll admit he was a surprise"

PERCIVAL PORC
1969-1973

This tombstone presents Percival as he would like to be
remembered.

However, in his existence here below he was the victim of the unjust
prejudices of his time and he died, at the age of four years, of
precocious frustration.

A poet who dreamt of flowering meadows, he was confined to the
mud of a pen ; a lover of music whose ambition was to become an
operatic singer, the public booed his first performance ; a romantic
who adored grace and beauty, he was affianced to his cousin Piggy.

We hope that this monument, conceived by him before his death,
is a true picture of his present life in the Elysian Fields.

"She ain't what she used to be"

Theodore's ancestors were puritans at heart, even before the missionaries came as far north as the Bearing Straits. He spent most of his youth trying to escape from all the girl-bears who were constantly pursuing him - until the day when, hidden among the pines, he saw Bruna taking her morning bath.

He decided then and there that when **she** got on her knees to him, he would not say no.

Bruna was courted by all the boy-bears of the region, but she found none to her liking - until the day when she glimpsed Theodore peering at her from amongst the pines. She decided then and there that when **he** got on his knees to her, she would not say no.

And they lived unhappily ever after.

Have you seen the new bottomless bathing suits ?

Helen Bovin was born on a farm near Angoulême, France, on the 1st of April, 1970 - which might explain a number of things.

Although she is more interested in the latest Parisian coiffures than in milk production, Farmer Bovin has installed her in a meadow of her own because he appreciates the qualities of her soul (it is the first time that he has really seen a cow's soul, its customary windows being too small).

Although aware of her charm, she is a little shy with strangers because she always suspects that you suspect that she is a joke.

Our photographer was very fortunate in getting this shot of
Professor Ely Ramson, who avoids publicity because he feels - quite
rightly - that neither he nor his theory of irrelativity could be
understood by the common man. Of course, a full-face portrait was
impossible. You will recall the tragic incident which occured the day
the *Daily News'* photographer asked him to smile.

Ulysses' revenge

Recently many of our readers have asked advice as to the most profitable investment of their savings - and their time.

Thinking that his opinion on the subject might be helpful, we consulted the brilliant financial expert, Ty Koon Jr., who suggests that you follow his example : i.e ; retire to your California estate, play golf, drink Bourbon, and dunk your troubles in the swimming pool.

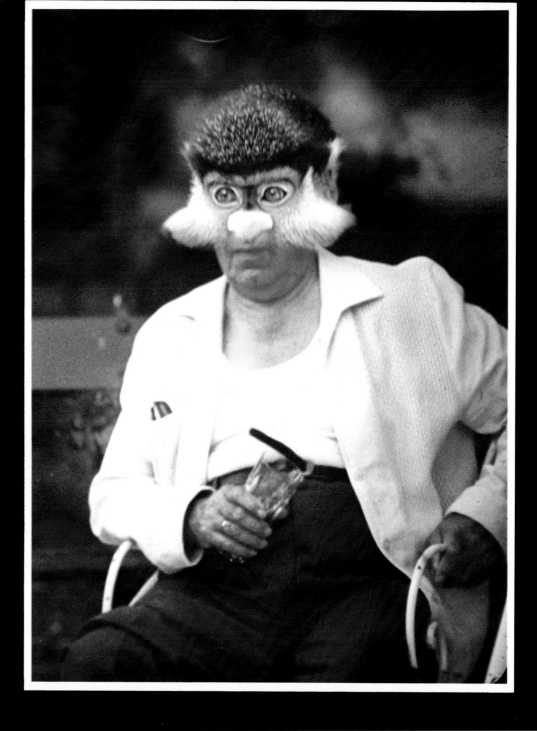

...and his partner M.A.G. Nate, vice-president of the M.T. Bank Corp., is attempting to forget his present financial difficulties by relaxing at his country estate. However, this solution of the problem seems inadequate, as he appears as blue as ever.

A hitherto unpublished study of Marcel Puce, recently discovered
among the papers of the late Baron de Katz. It is believed to have
been taken at the latter's country estate, where the famous
author was a guest during the summer of 1904.

He had just completed "The Sweet Cat Gone" and was recovering
from one of his more severe attacks of hyperaestheticism.

The great dramatist, New Jersey Williams, says that the superb realism of his plays is due to his living among, and like, the people who are to become his unforgettable characters.

"Where's that scissor-happy barber?
I'd like to kill him!
*And I **will** kill the next one of the boys who calls me "Butterfly."*

Dear Edith,

*On Saturday we were all herded up to the Place du Tertre (Montmartre).
Where the artists are, you know.*

*When you come over, you **must** have one of them do your portrait.
Such marvellous drawings! Such perfect likenesses! You will be
amazed when I show you mine..*
                                                                    Love,
                                                                Gwendolyn

Dear Mother,

Paris, France, is not at all like Paris, Texas. One of the differences is that here there are out-of-door cafés where one can sit for hours.

Grace and I went to the famous "Deux Magots" yesterday to watch the exotic characters go by. You see the strangest people! It's better than a show.

How is everything back on the farm?

Love to all,
Louise

A vegetarian diet is not only good, but good for you.
Economical too.

"I am aware that human beings consider themselves more intelligent than canines but, personally, I find them - if not exactly stupid - at least extremely unobservant.

The proof is that during the eight years that we have lived together, my mistress has never noticed that when I pretend to sleep, I keep one eye open.

It is hard to believe."

The appointment of W. Warren Beekly as Chief National Avenging-Angel is to be applauded. He is outstandingly qualified for the post by long years of experience and by his sincere love of the profession.

In spite of his age, he is always on the alert and ready to serve.

*"I was very flattered when a student organisation proposed that
I lead one of their demonstrations, insisting that my voice would be an
invaluable asset.*

*I still do not understand for what cause they are demonstrating;
but I am sure that it is a good one – they are such nice young people.*

*However, I was wrong to accept, because I now feel strongly that
I am somehow letting them down."*

"When I came home yesterday, I again found the house in disorder, the dinner not even started, and Fifi sitting at the front door.

This time I accused her bluntly of wanting to attract the attention of the trotters-by. (As a matter of fact, she had actually wagged her tail at Dachsy Thompson).

When I reproved her for her unladylike conduct, she said she had not even seen him.

Is she lying?

Is it possible that she does not see anything?"

A primitive tribe, deep in the jungles of northern Lepidoptera, still worships the ancient God of Fertility, but this is probably the first time that the ceremony of purification has been caught by the camera. The - in this case, ripe - virgin is genuflecting before the spirit of Toto-Tutu, asking his benediction on her forthcoming solo flight.

"You, there in the mirror!
Why are you pensive?
Why are you sad?
Your eyes are green and luminous. your hands are pale and slight.
Your hair is long and lustrous. your whiskers stiff and white.
What is the secret, sister?
Why am I pensive?
Why am I sad?

*"My wife would stop complaining if
she only realized how exhausting it is
to go through the help-wanted advertisements
every day."*

"Isabel and I have been inseparable since our early lambhood,
gamboling in the same pasture, sharing our most intimate secrets;
but now, on the threshold of sheephood, she has somehow changed.

She no longer listens to my confidences — her attention is elsewhere,
particularly when there are rams around.

Perhaps my mother is right in calling her a bad influence.

I don't know what to think."

One day an ostrich came to the conclusion that hiding one's head in the sand was not the way to get the most out of life. So he decided to move to the city, to see and be seen.

Two problems presented themselves. The first was his personal appearance. (He had shaken the sand out of his hair and had a good look at himself in the mirror). The second was that he had no means of earning a livelihood in the metropolis, certainly not enough capital to buy a business. But he refused to be discouraged. He said to himself:
"Ugliness is no obstacle because a man is judged by his accoutrements. If I am dressed richly in scarlet and gold, all will think me beautiful. And if I have no fruit or shoes or jewels to sell — well then, I shall sell water."
And so it came to pass.

Portrait of a Self-Made Dog

At the annual meeting of the Rotary Club of Doghasset, L.I., Dwight L. Shepherd was presented with the award of Leading Citizen for his invaluable contribution to the happiness and peace of mind of his compatriots.

He is the inventor and producer of the ST. ANTHONY DOG TAG, which has brought consolation to all who were haunted by the fear of losing their masters - and who among us was not ?

An orphan, educated at the S.P.C.A., his outstanding success is due solely to his own initiative, to his complete devotion to the industry, and to his always impeccable appearance.

When asked by our reporter if he was considering retirement, he admitted, in confidence, that it was impossible, because he had discovered that instead of owning his business, his business owned him.

Topolino

Cordially yours,

Topolino